THIS BOOK

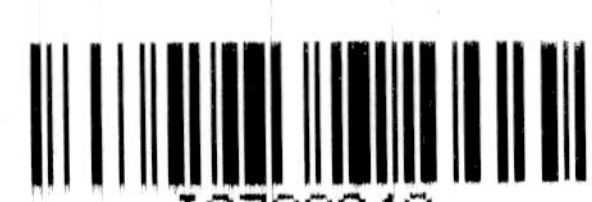

BELONG TO

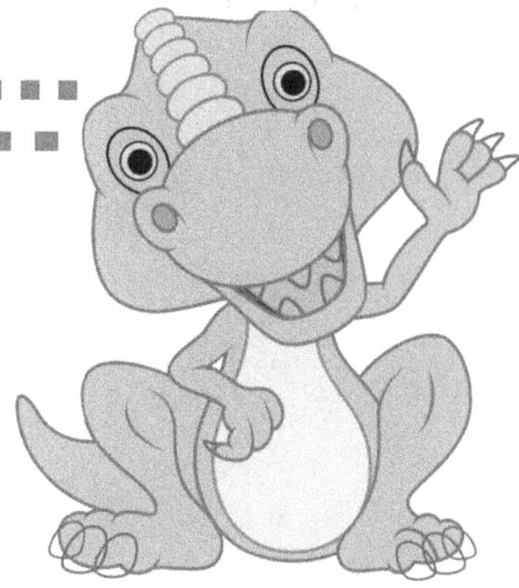

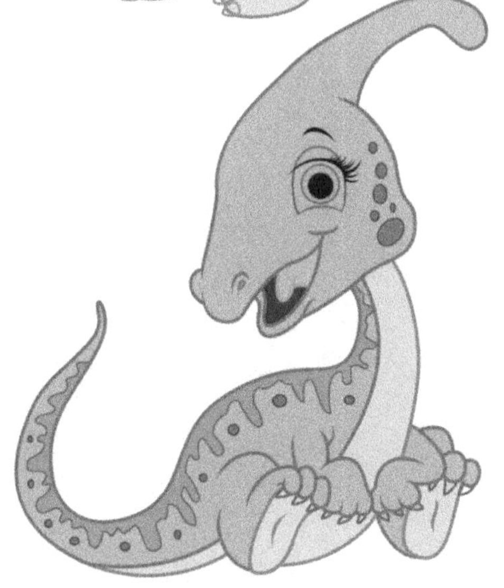

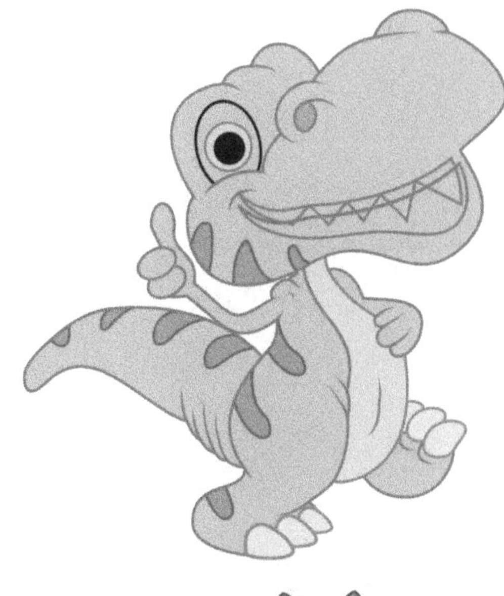

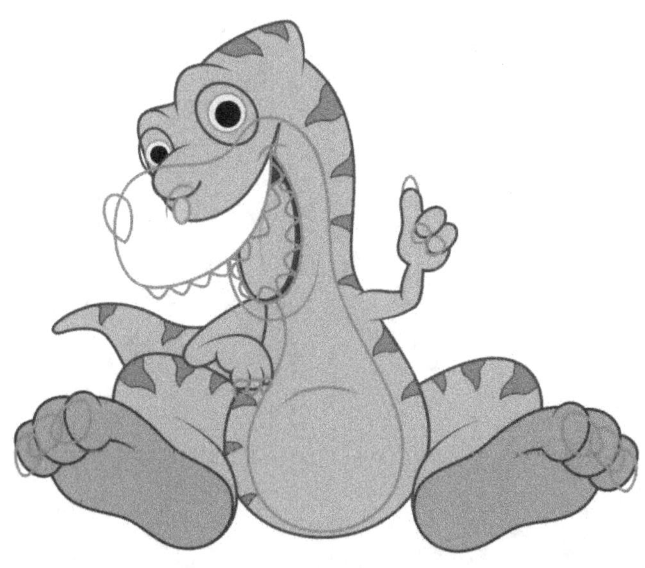

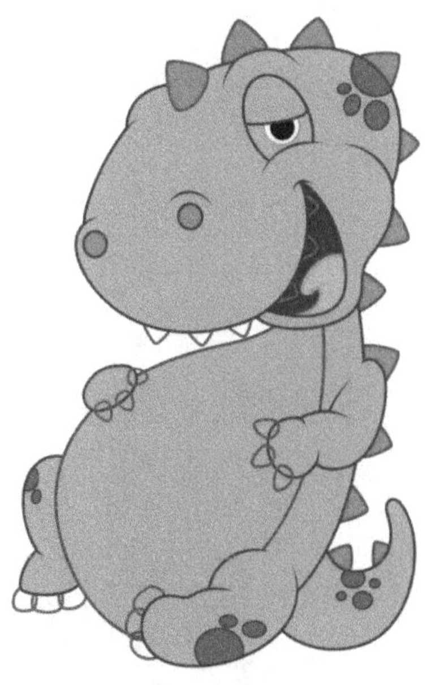

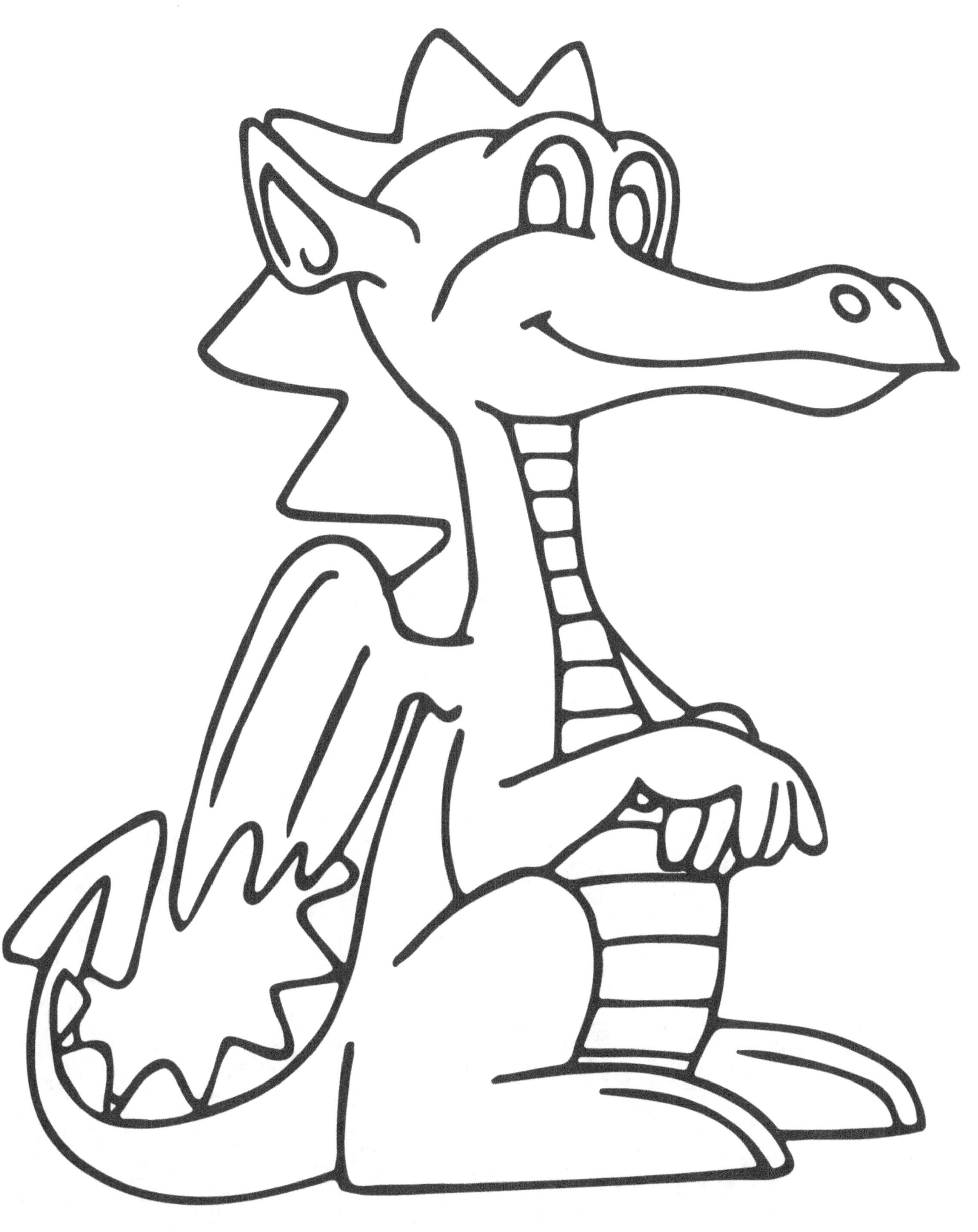

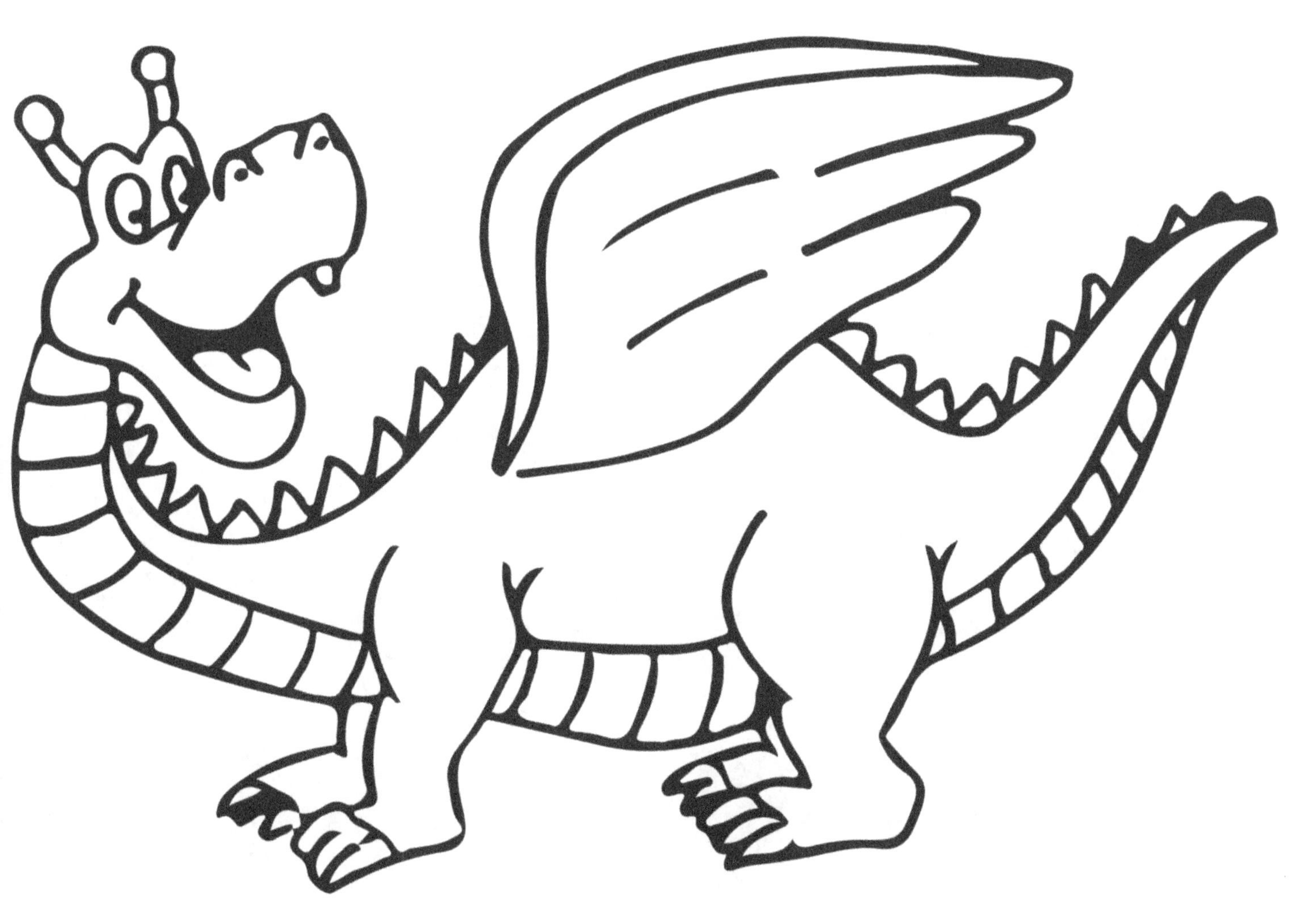

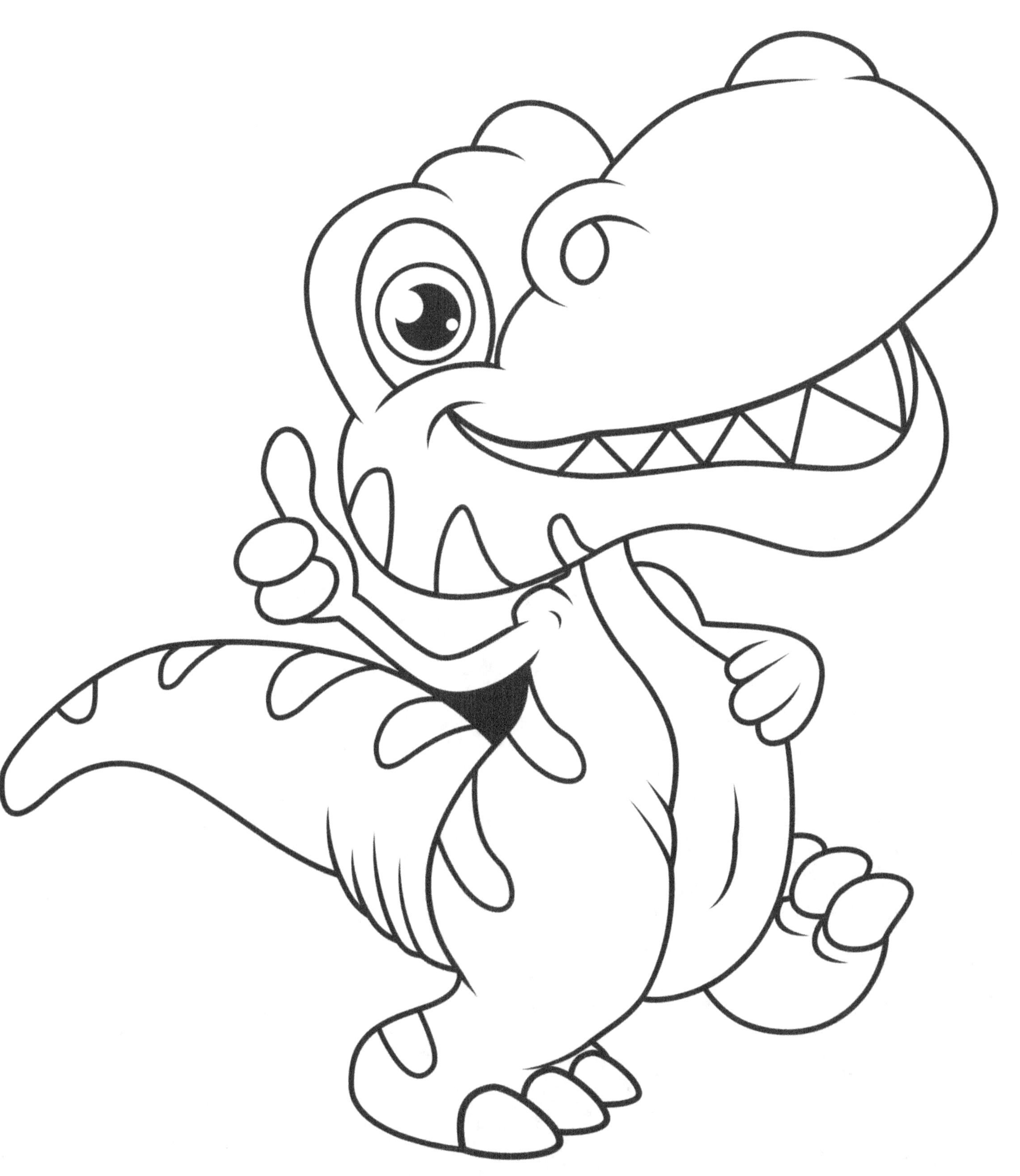

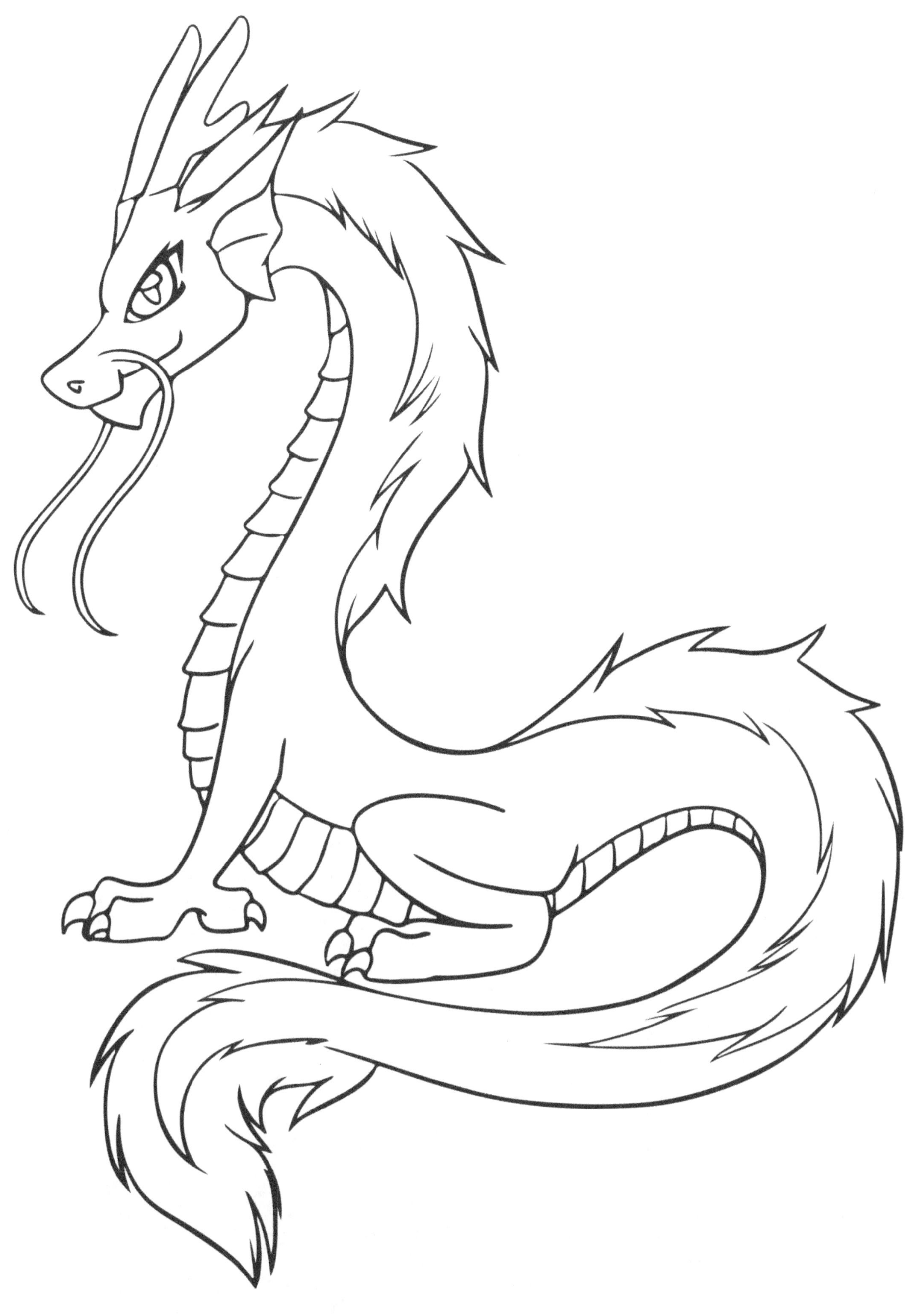

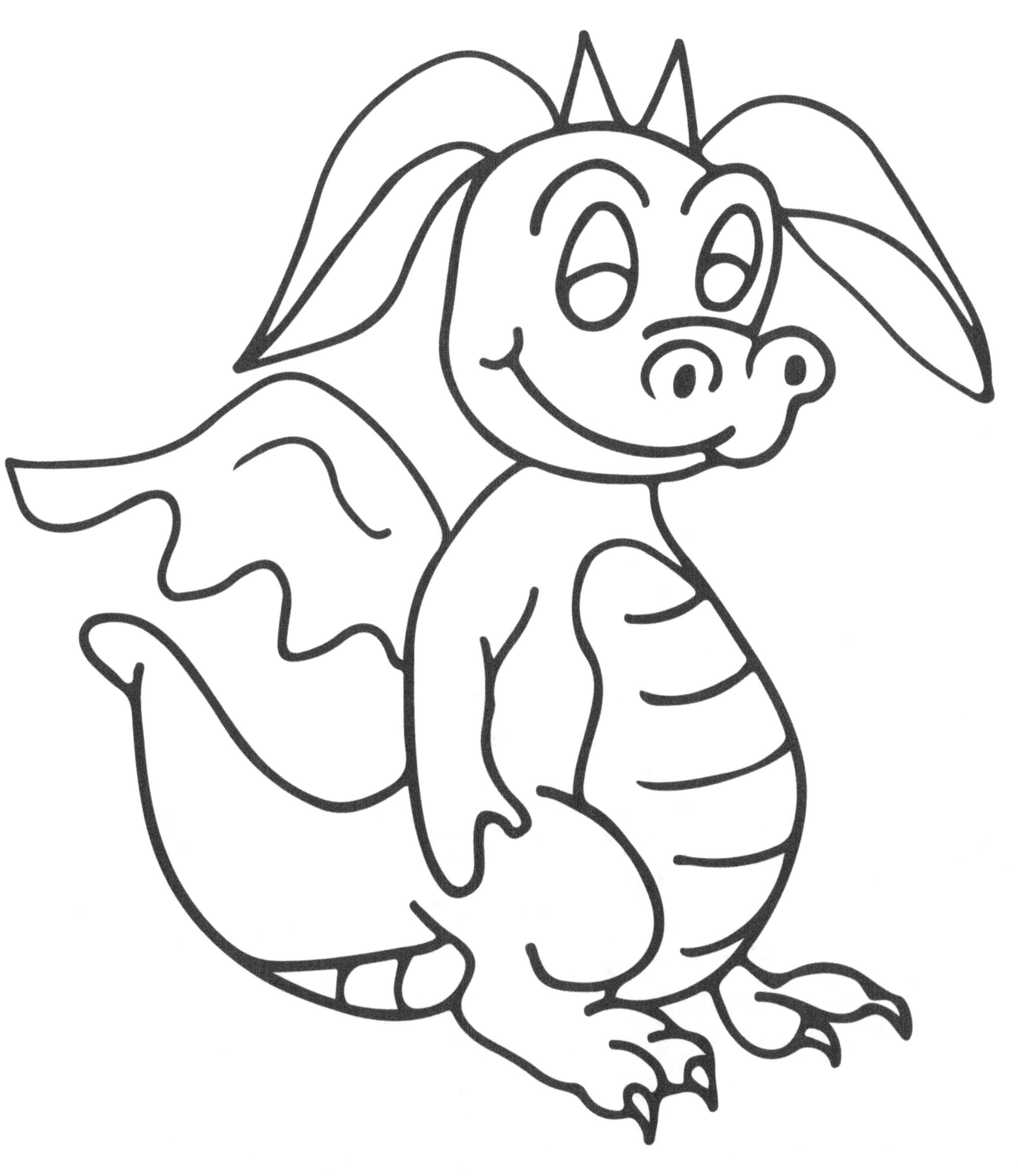

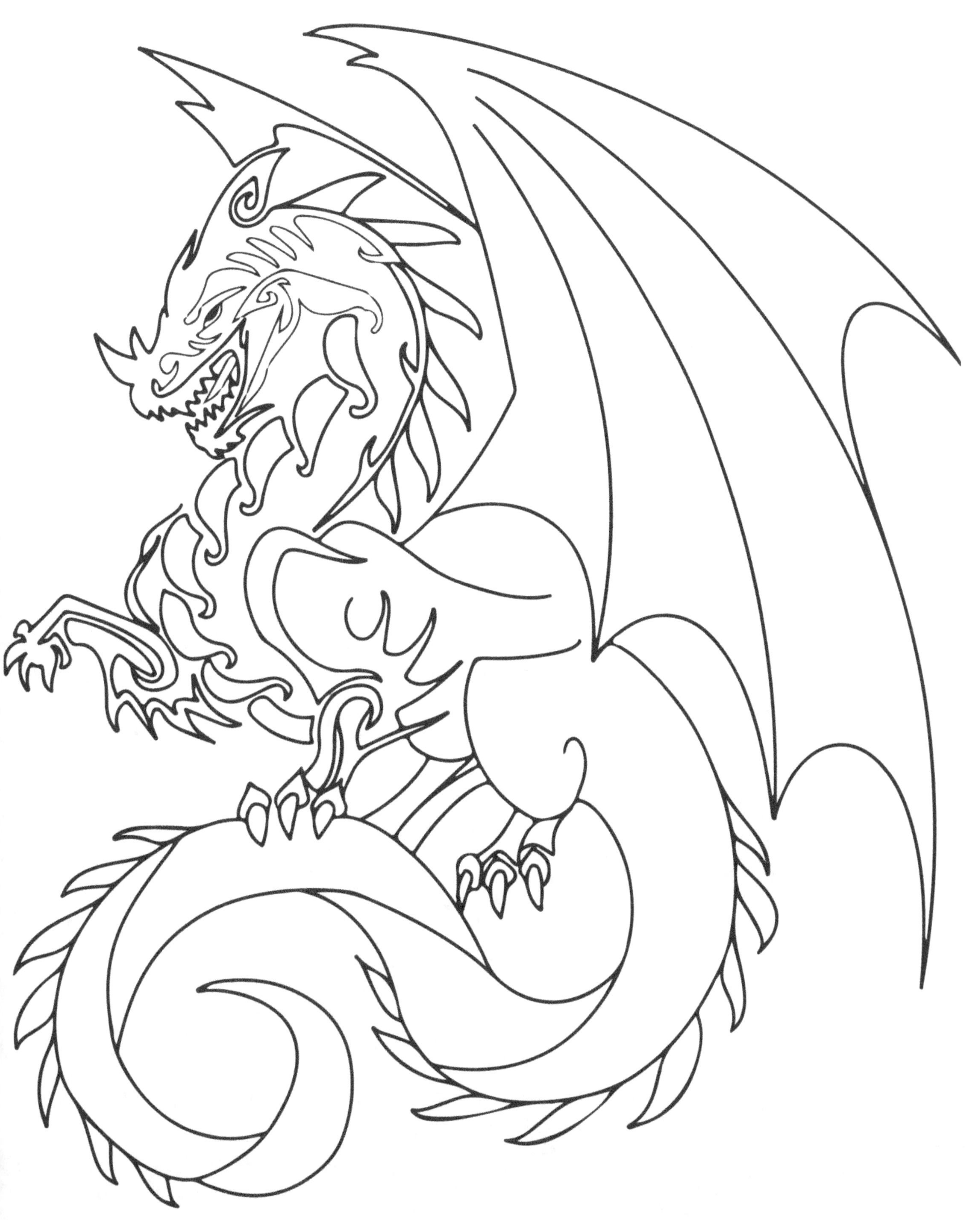

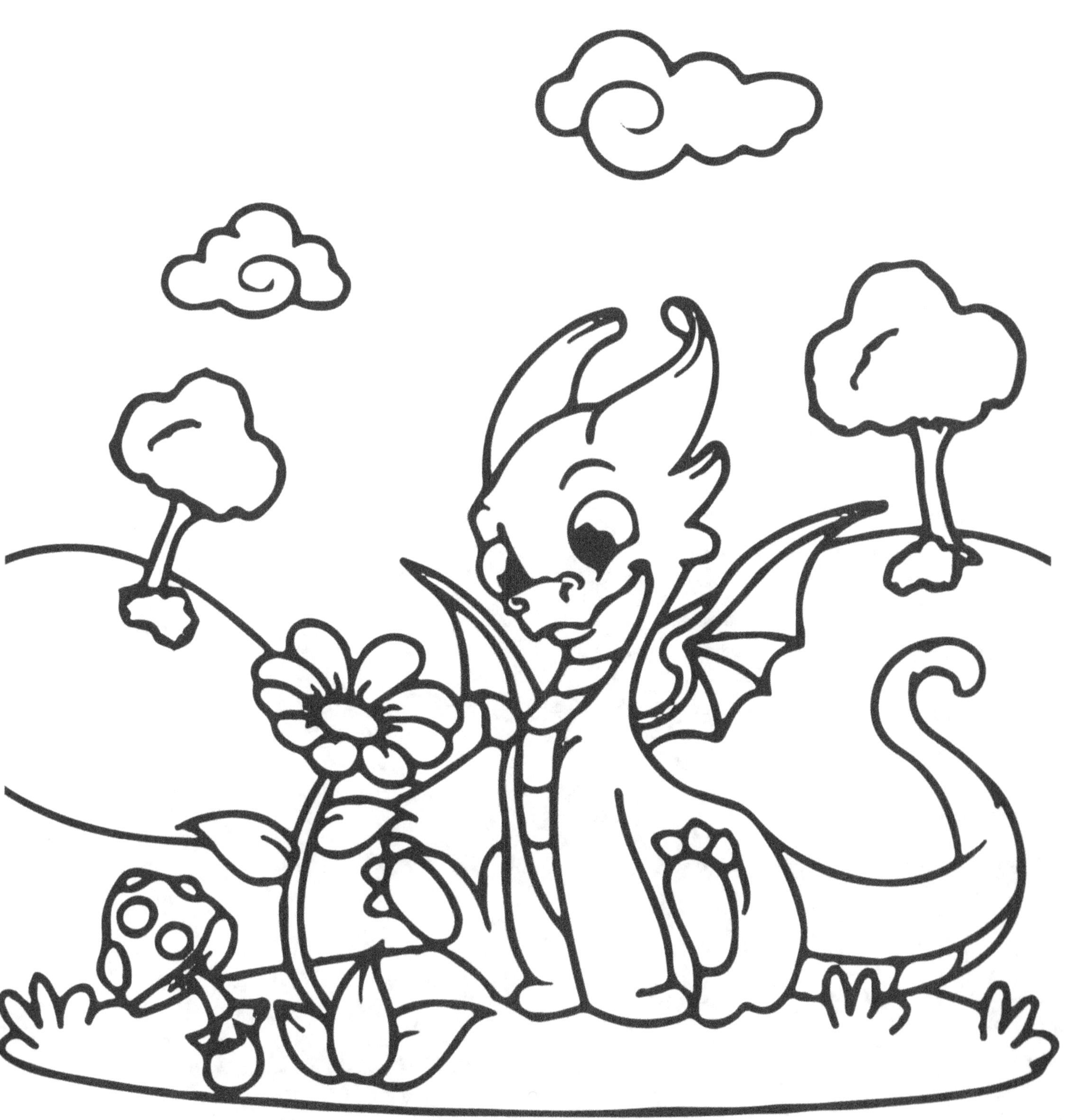

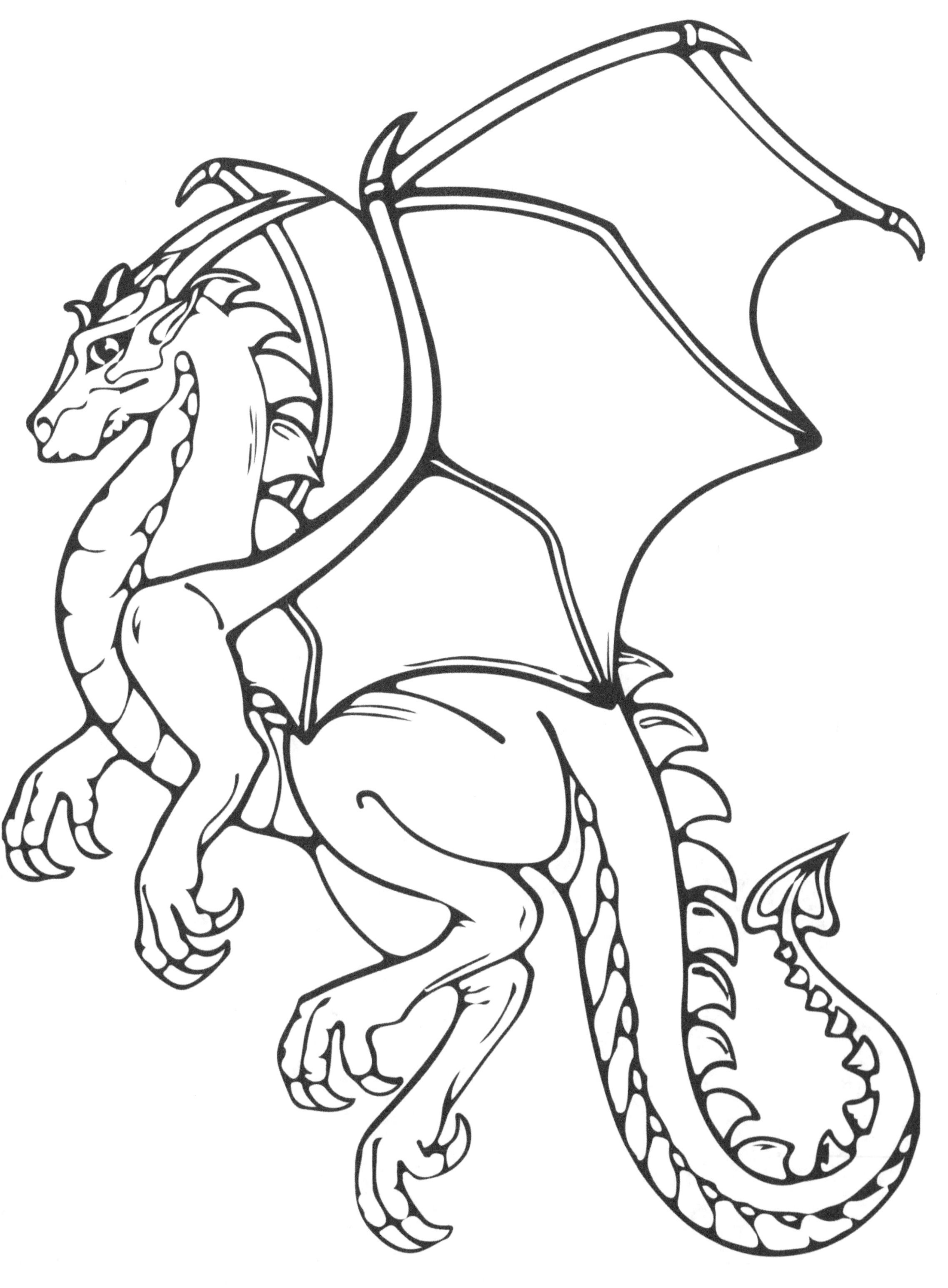

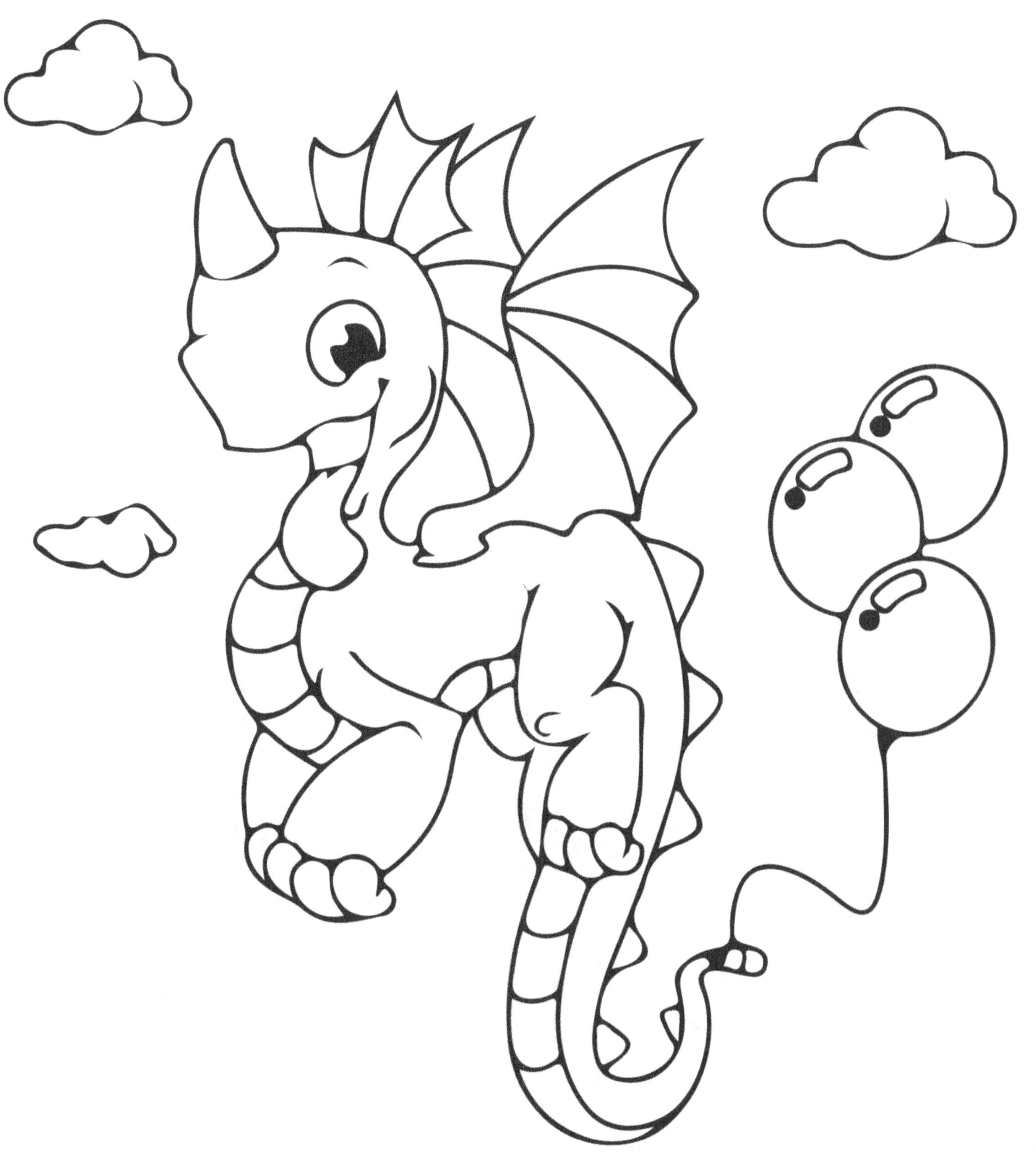

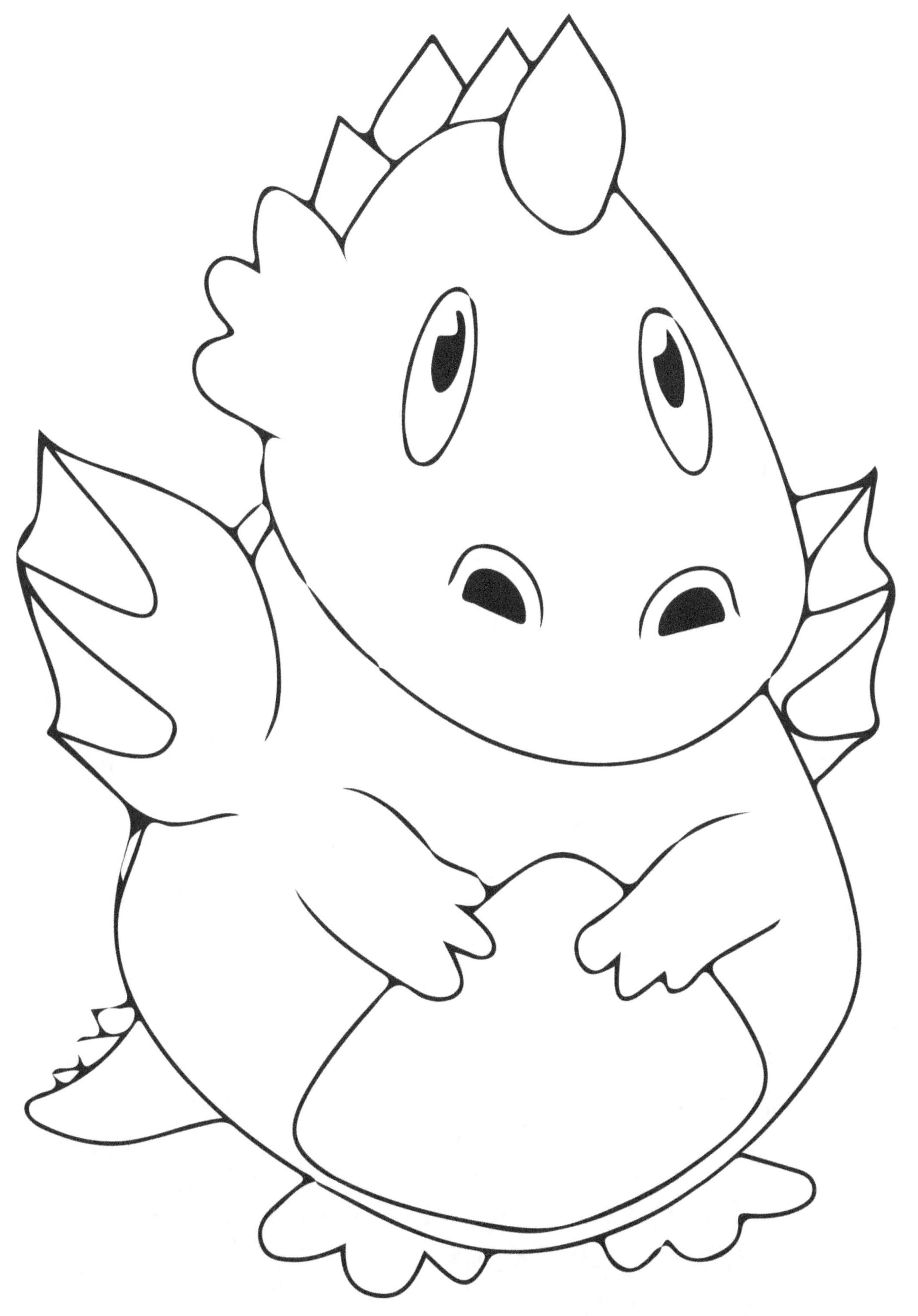

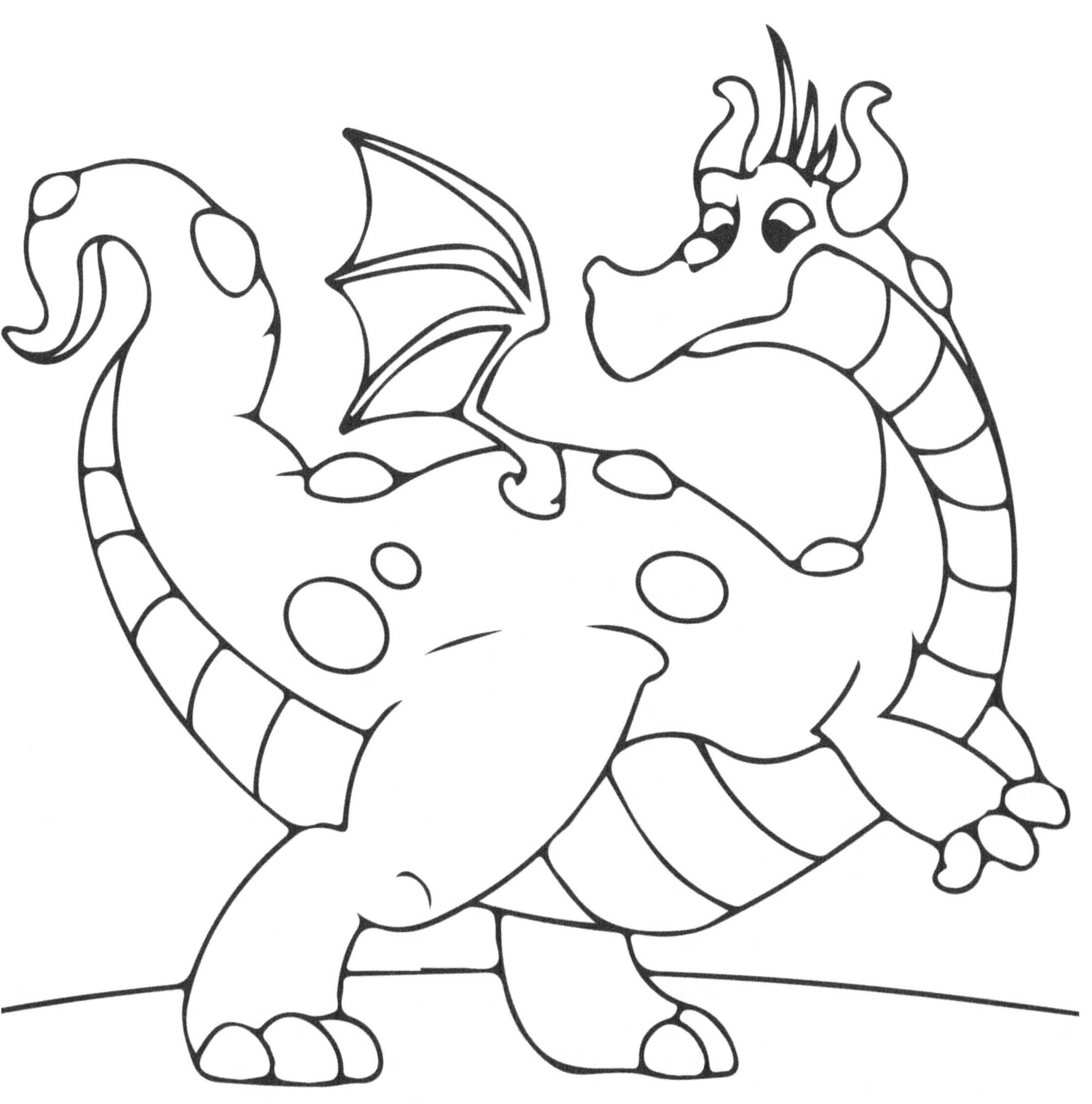

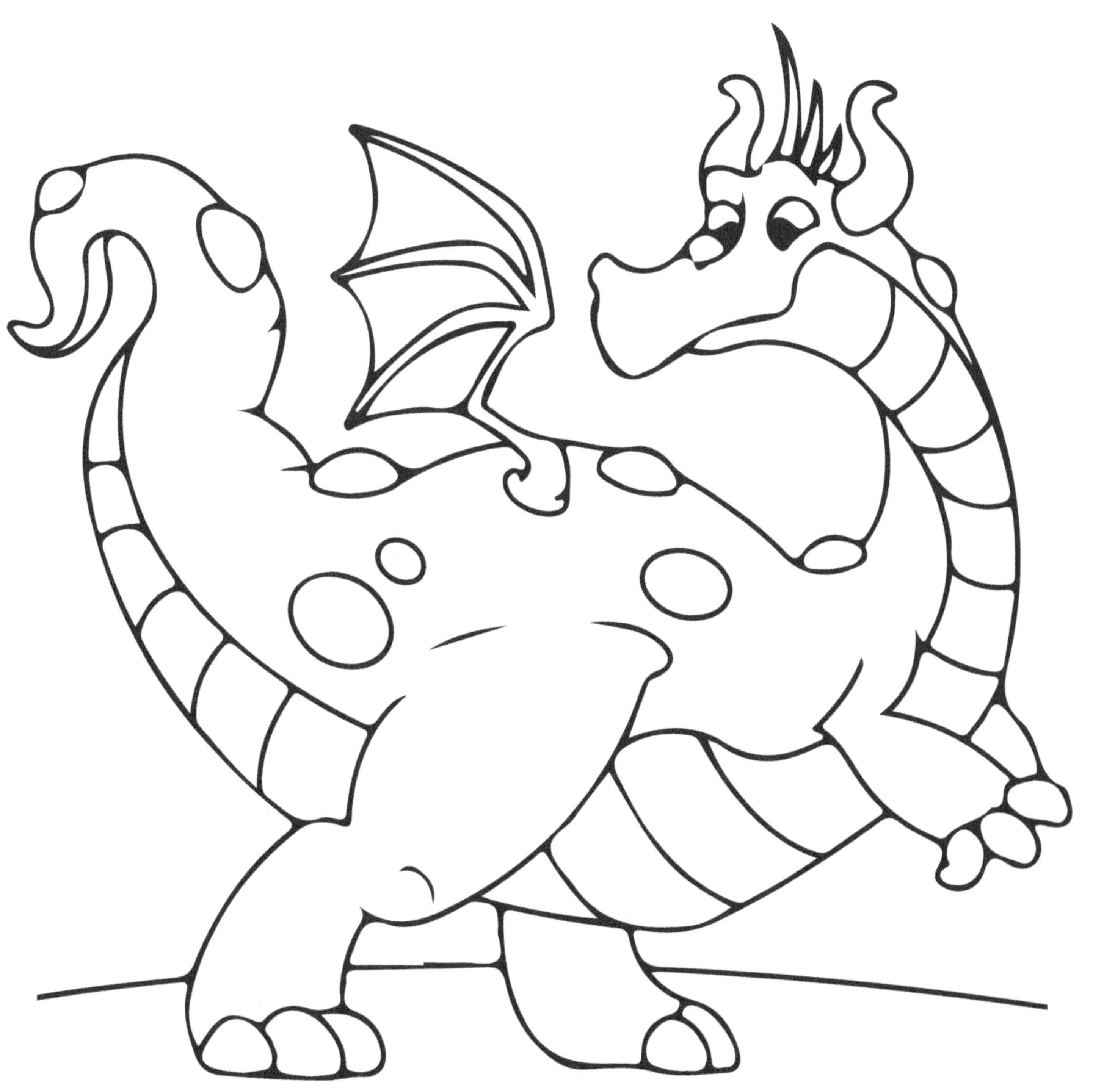

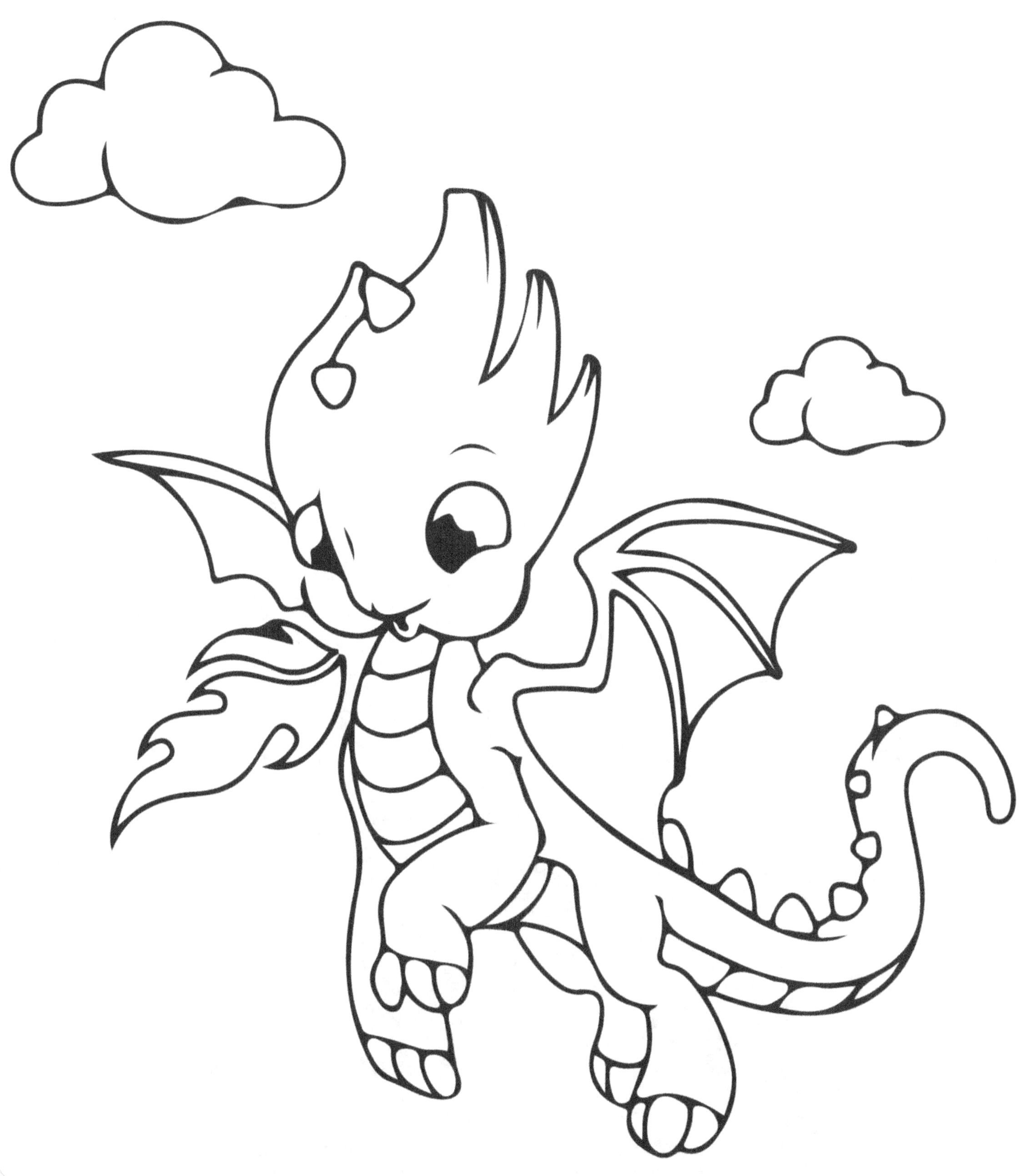

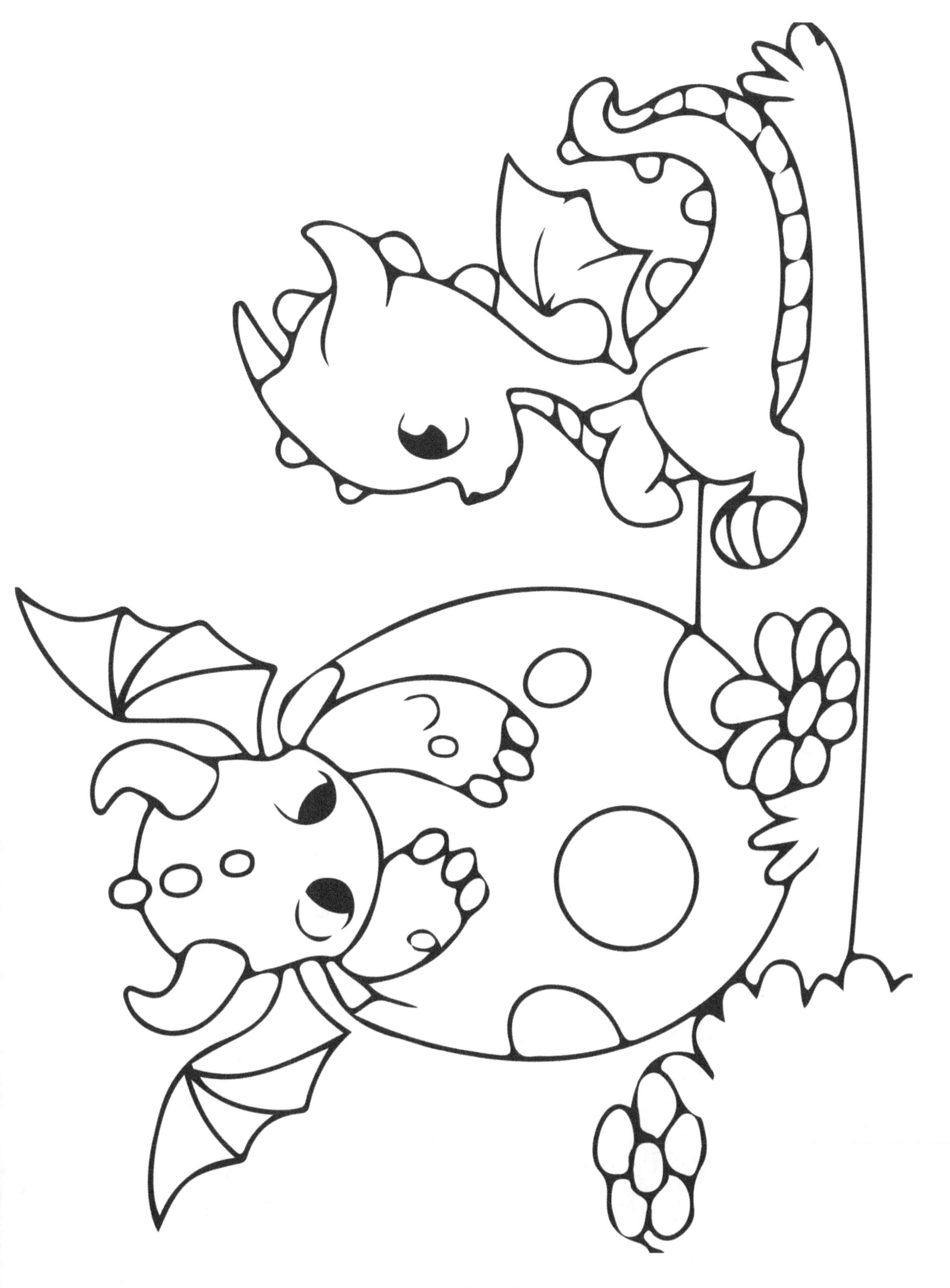

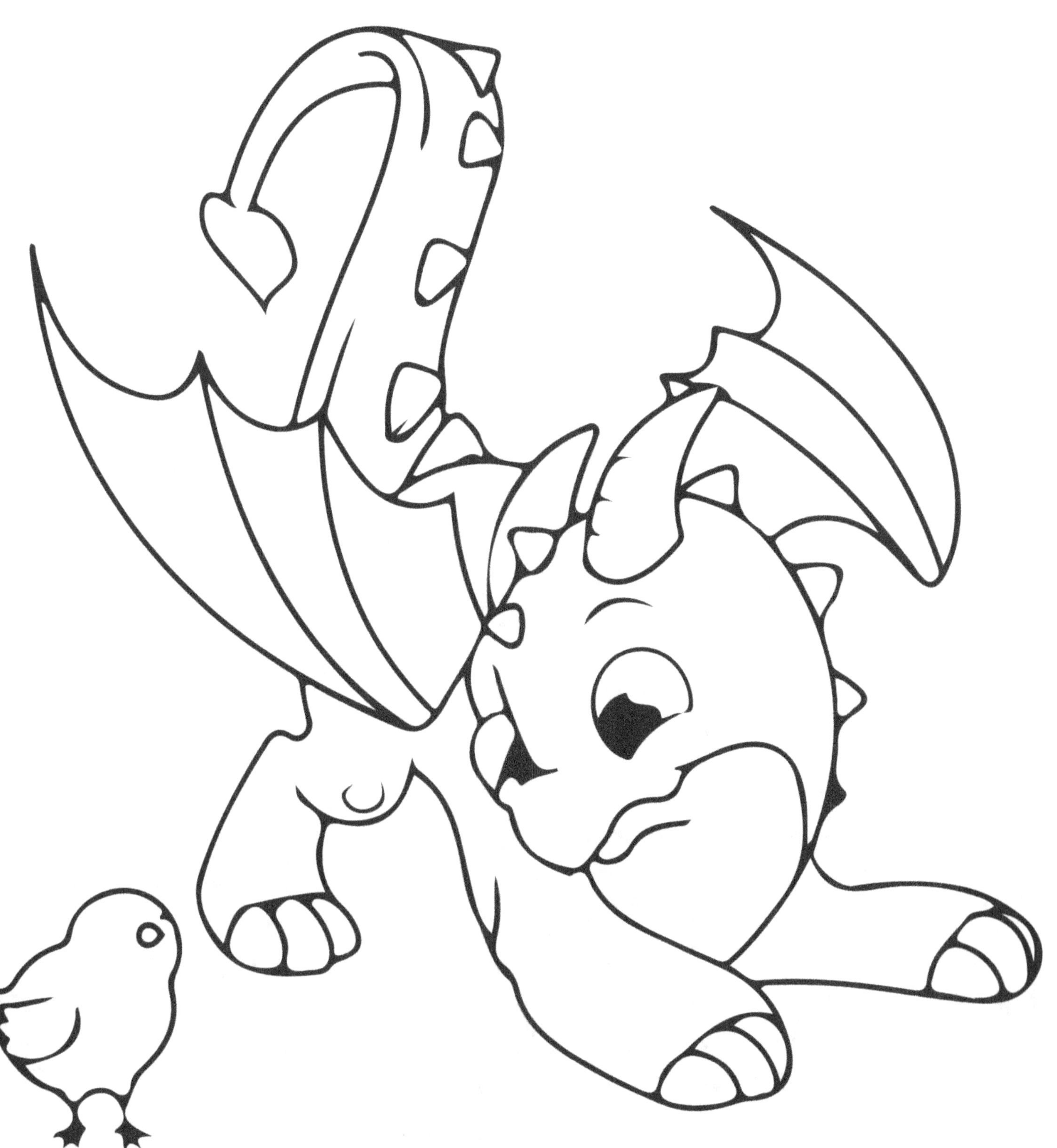

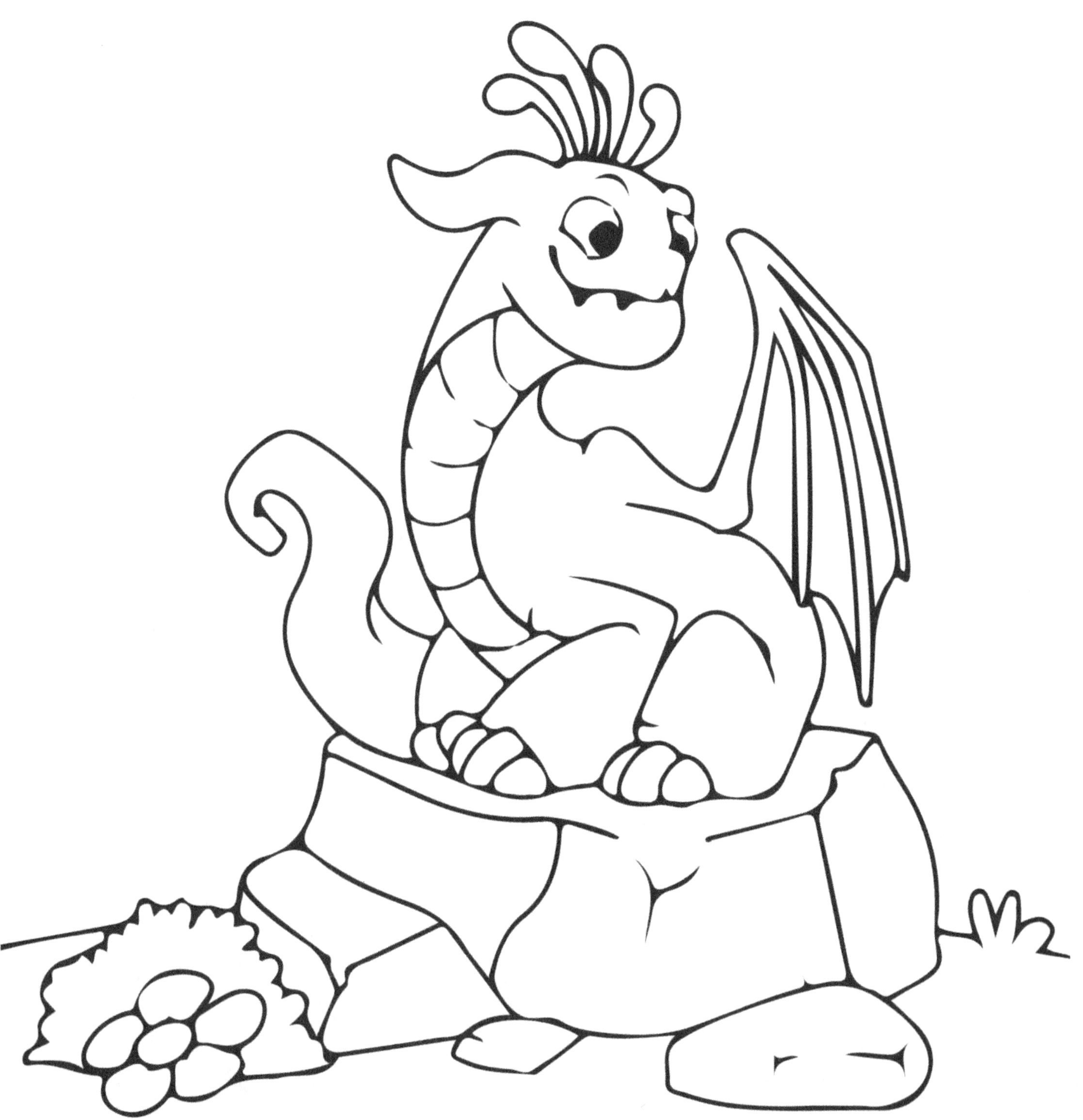

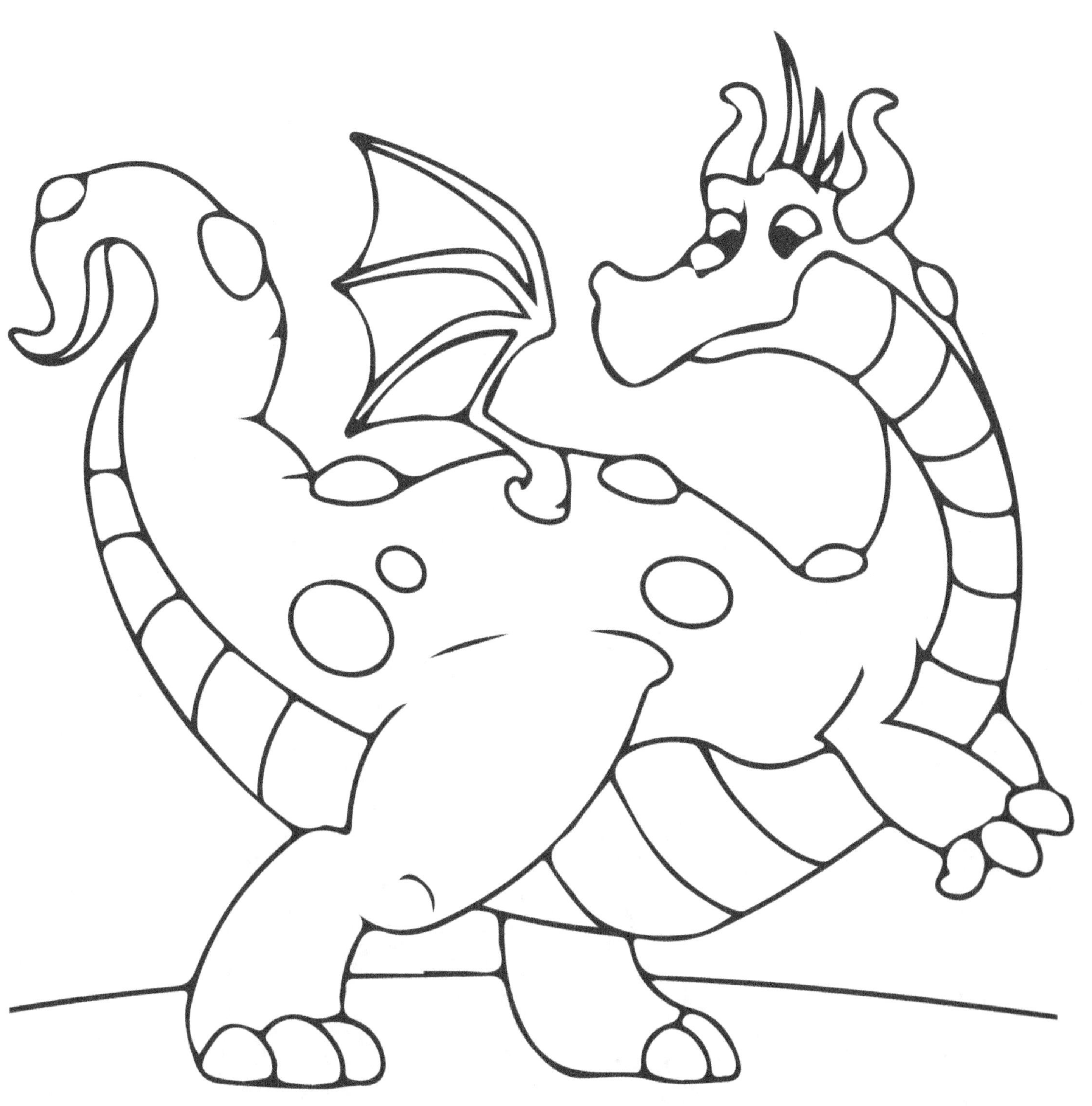

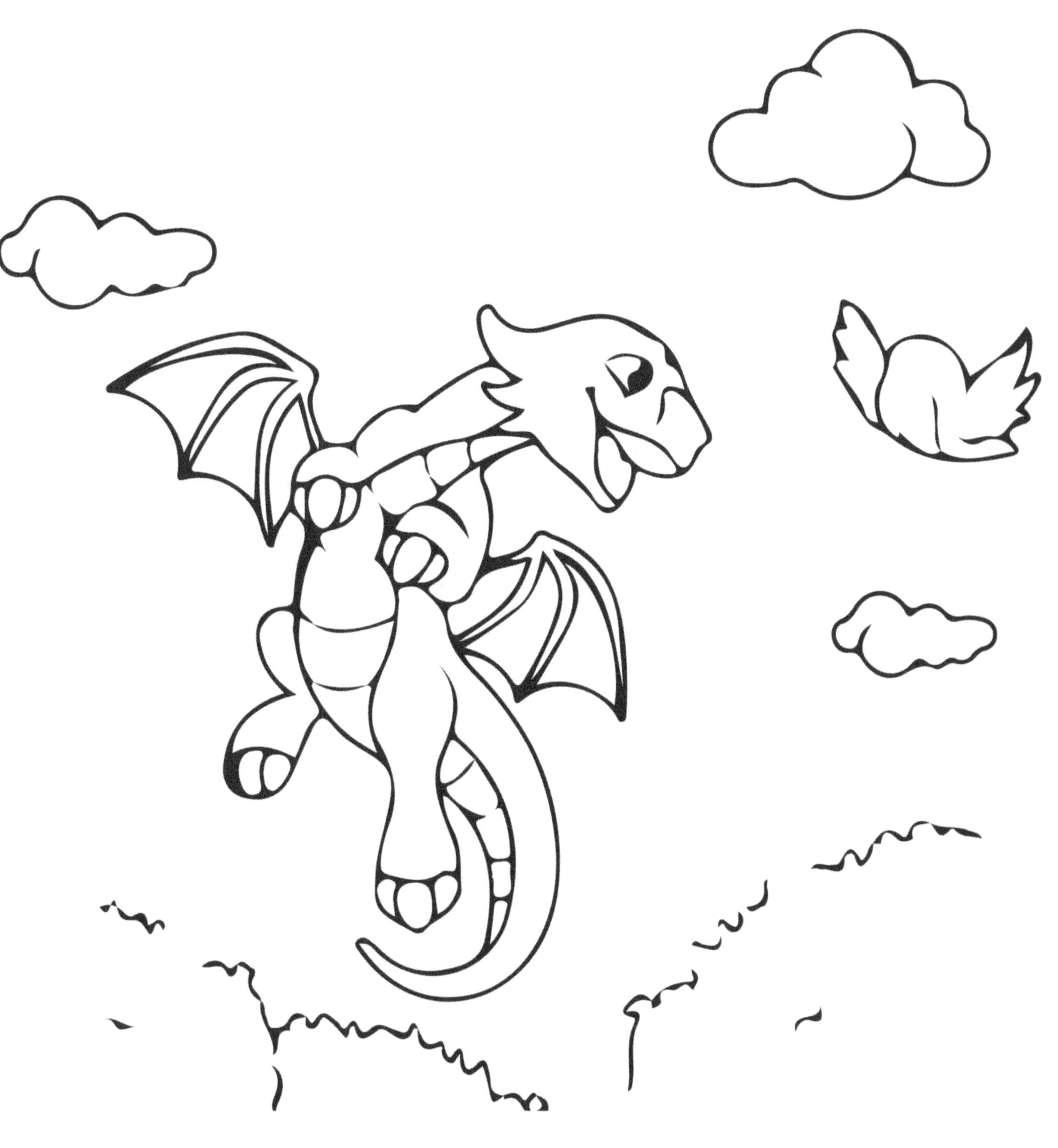

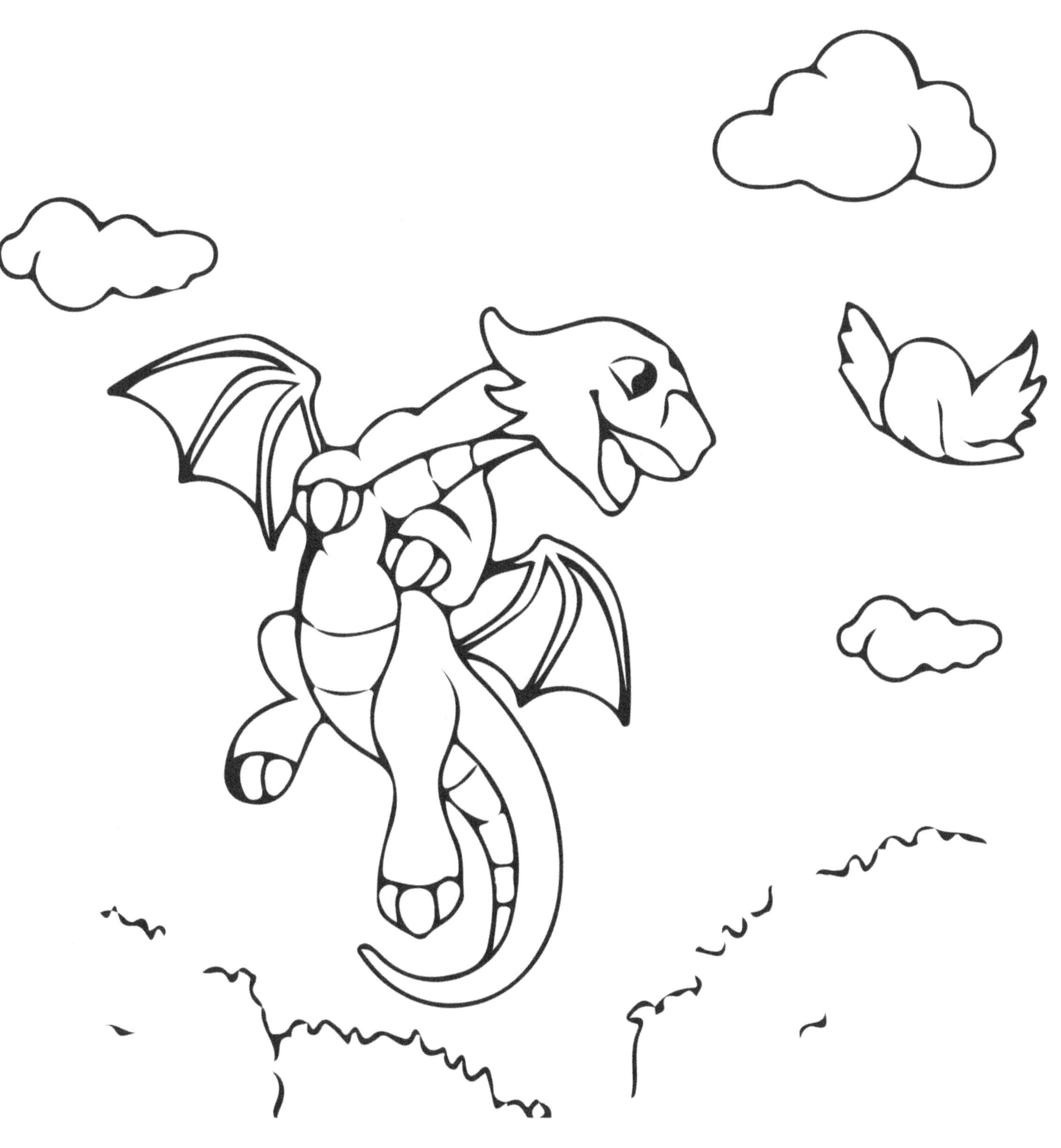

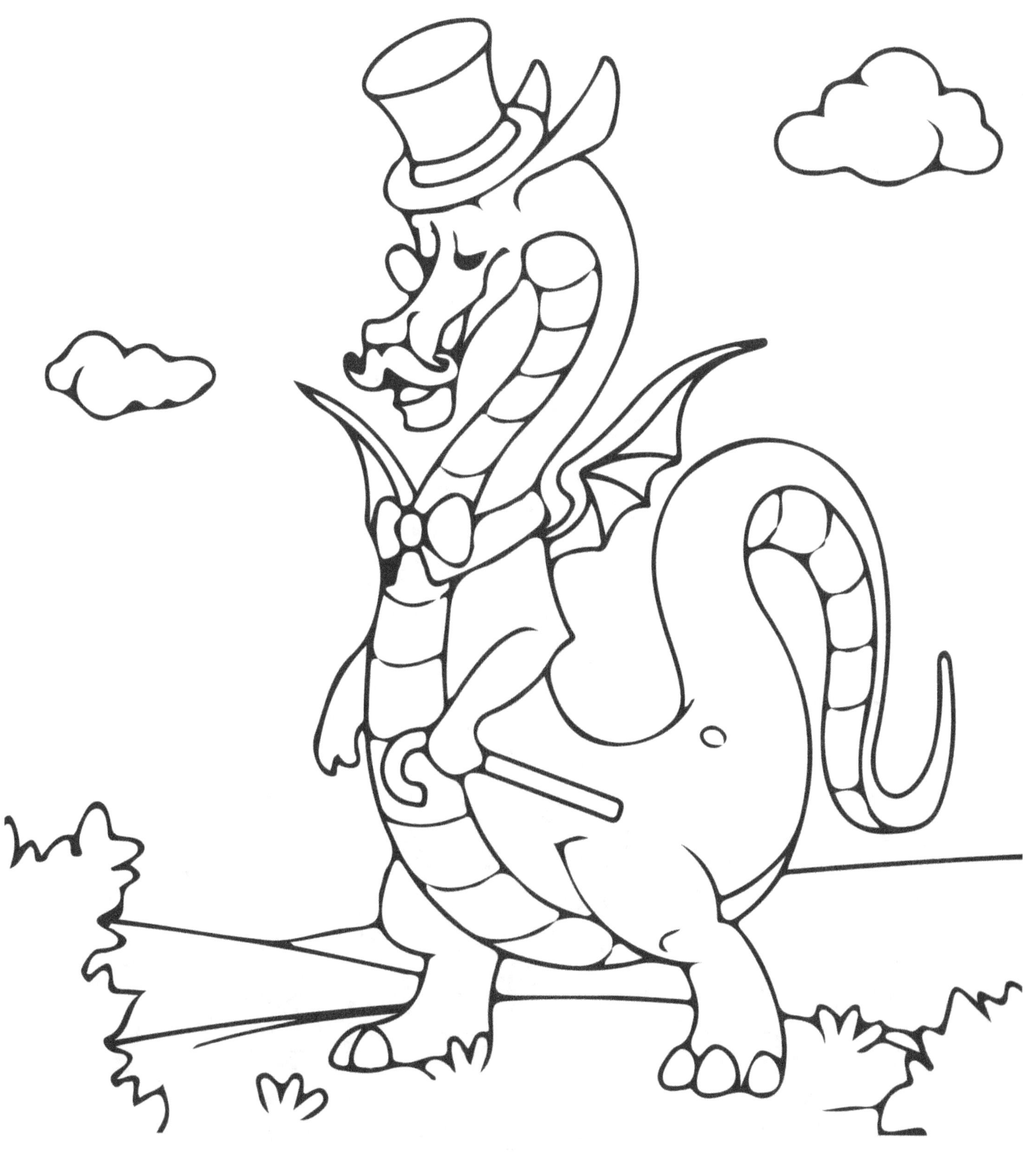

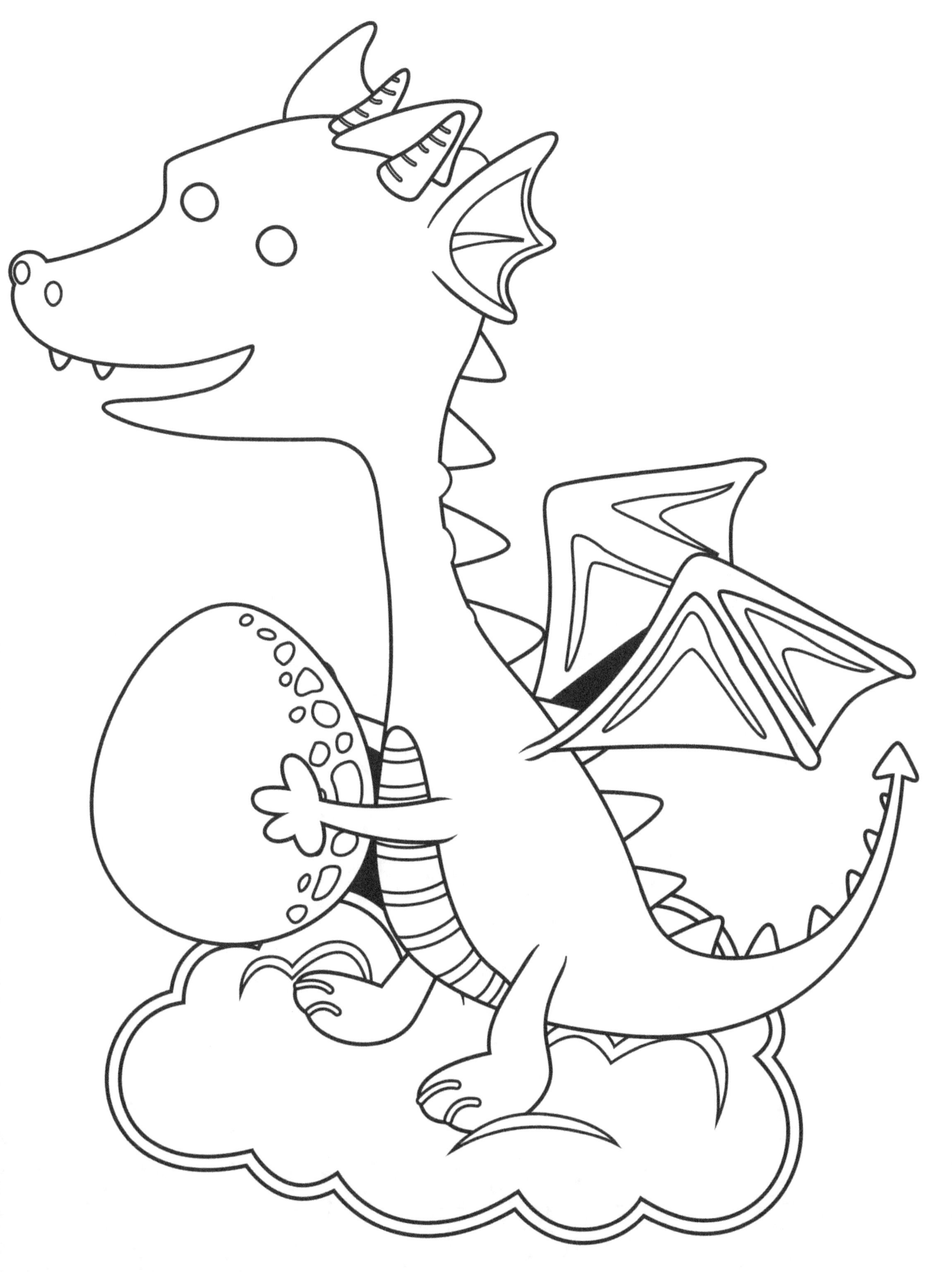

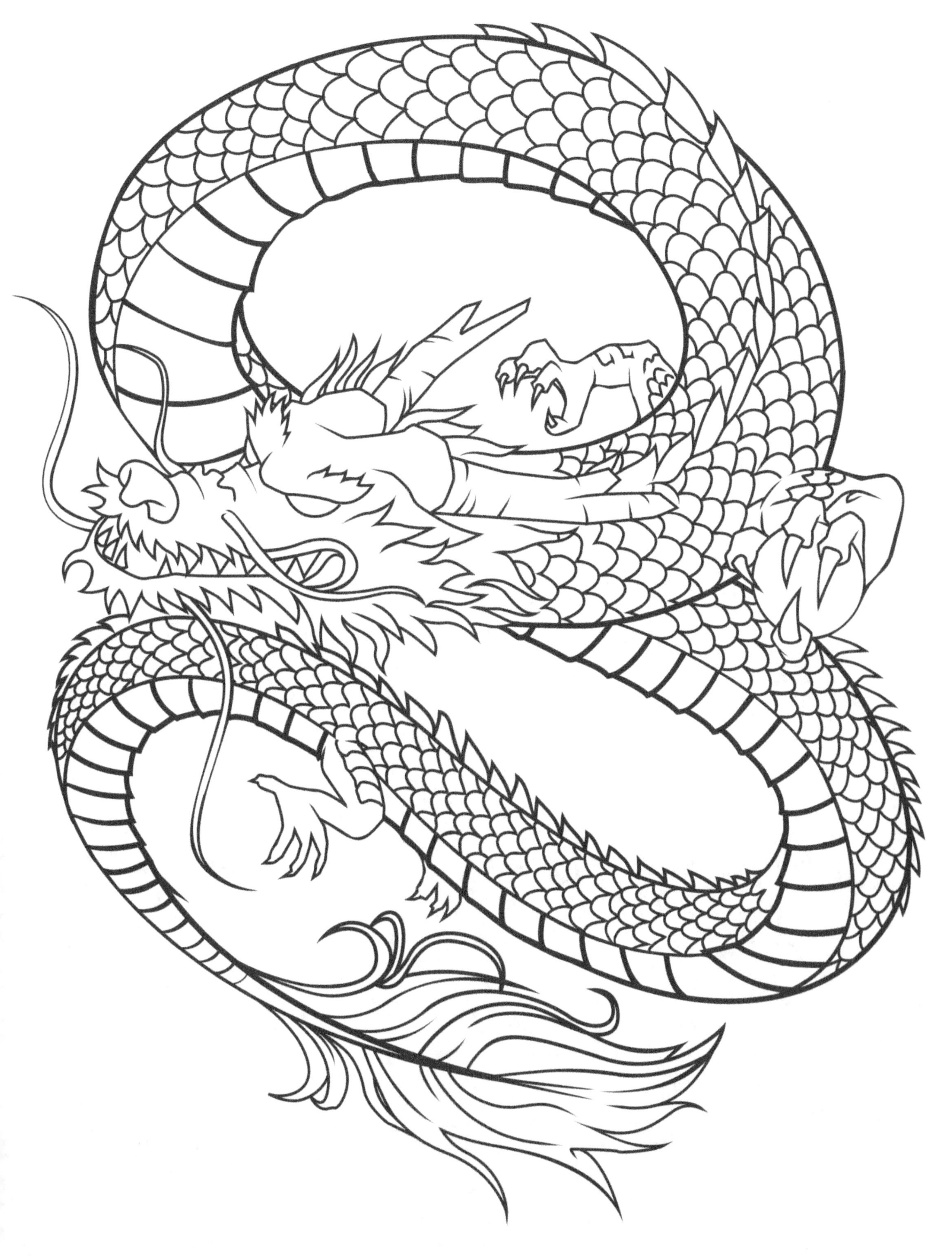

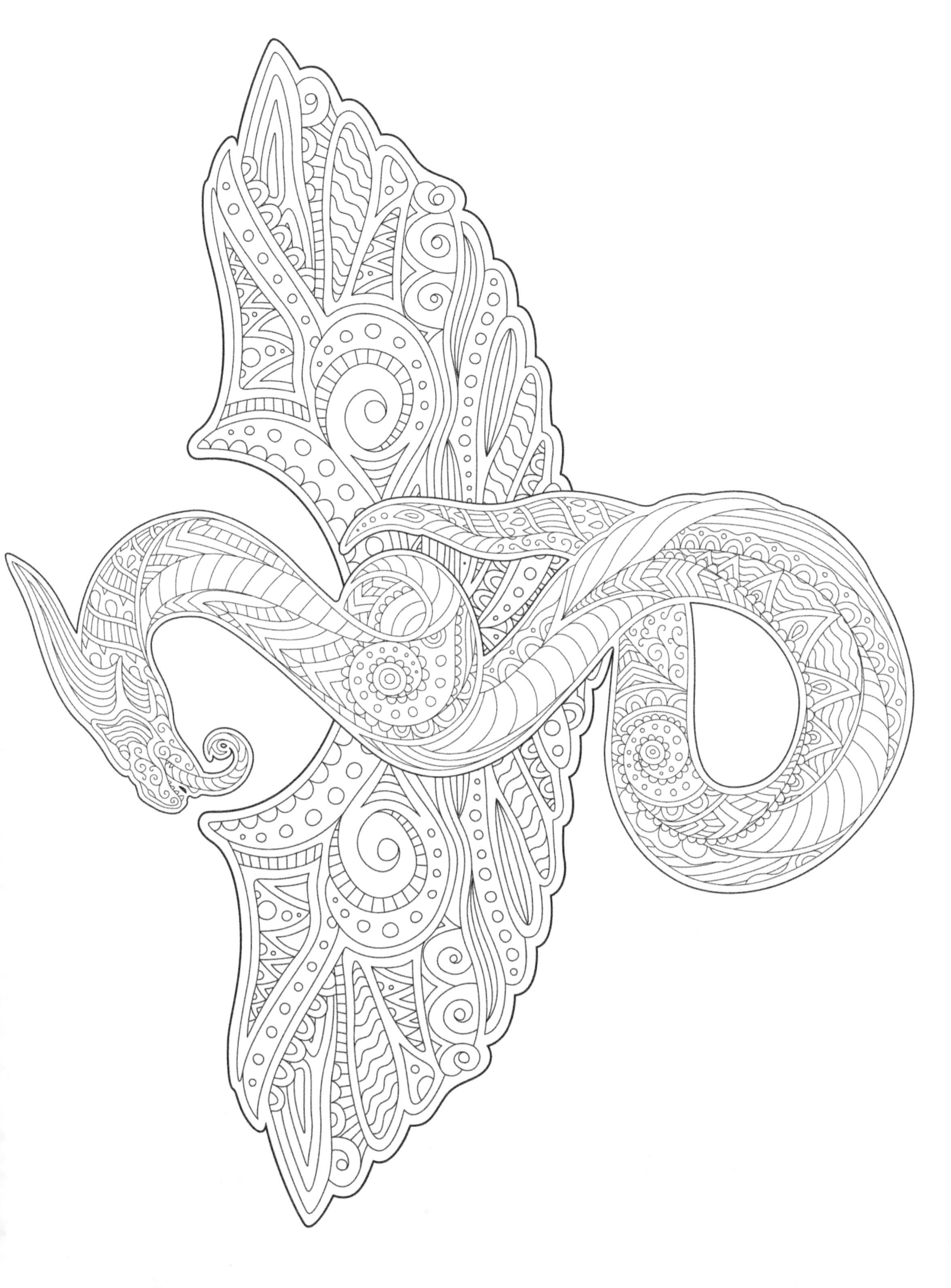

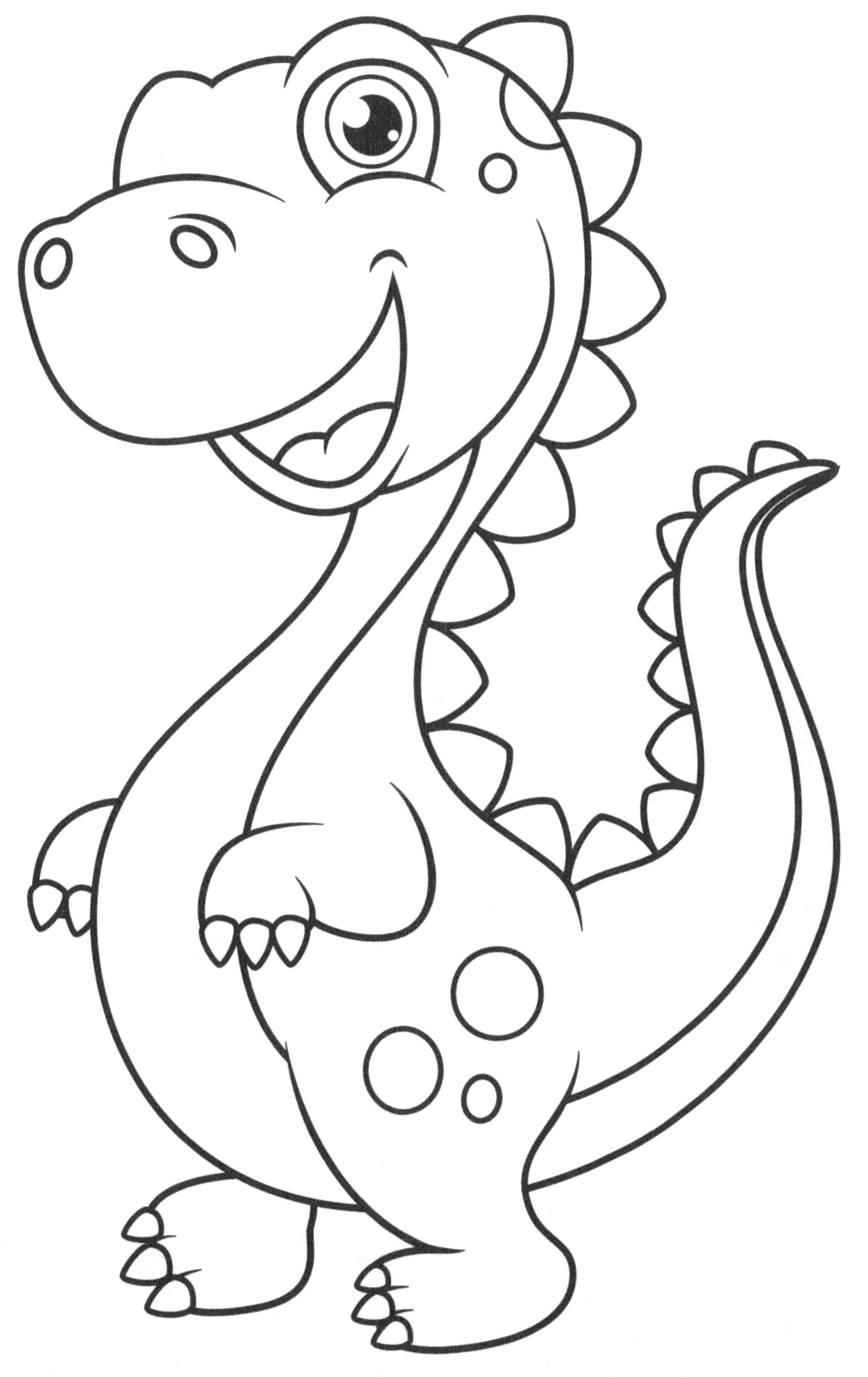

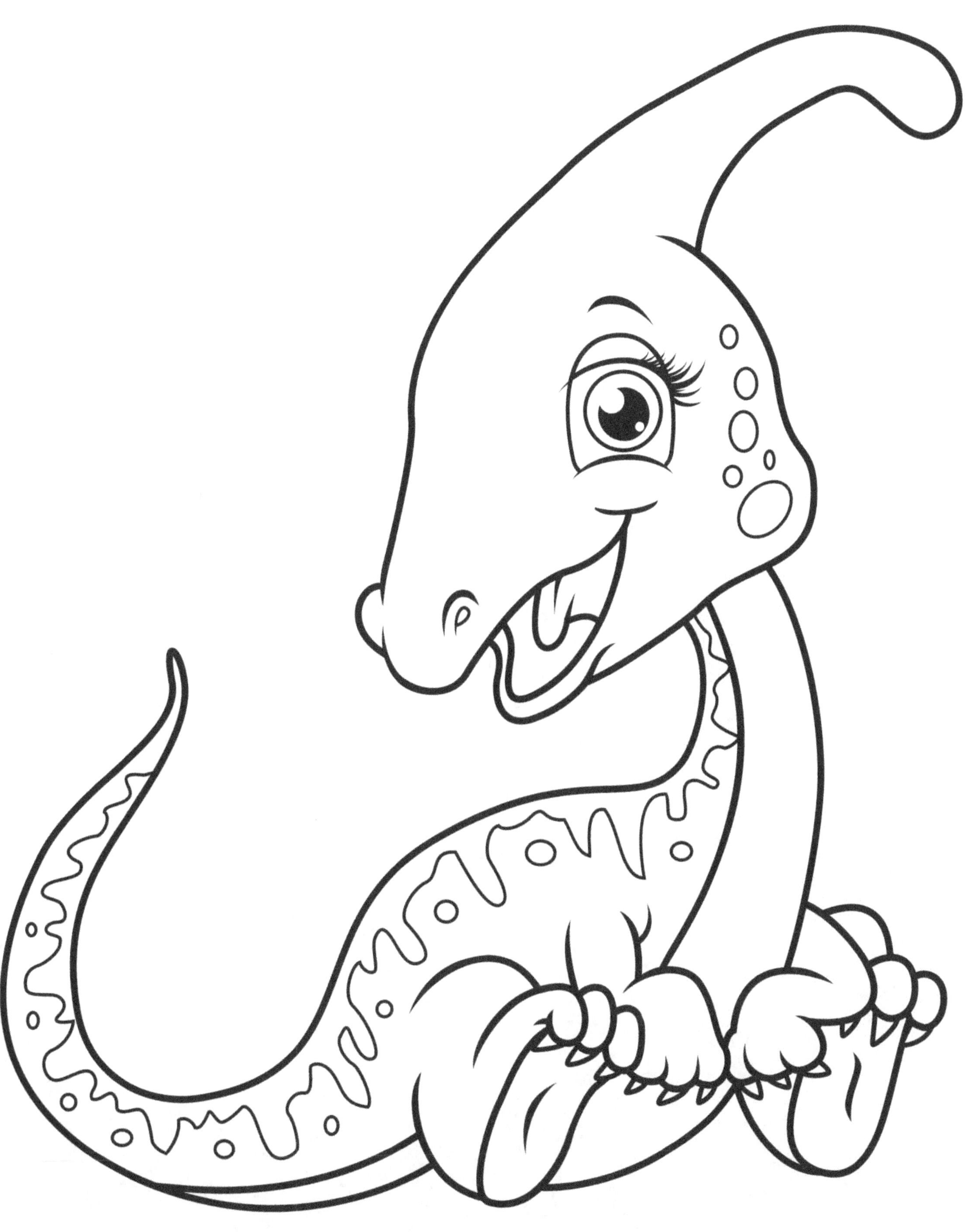

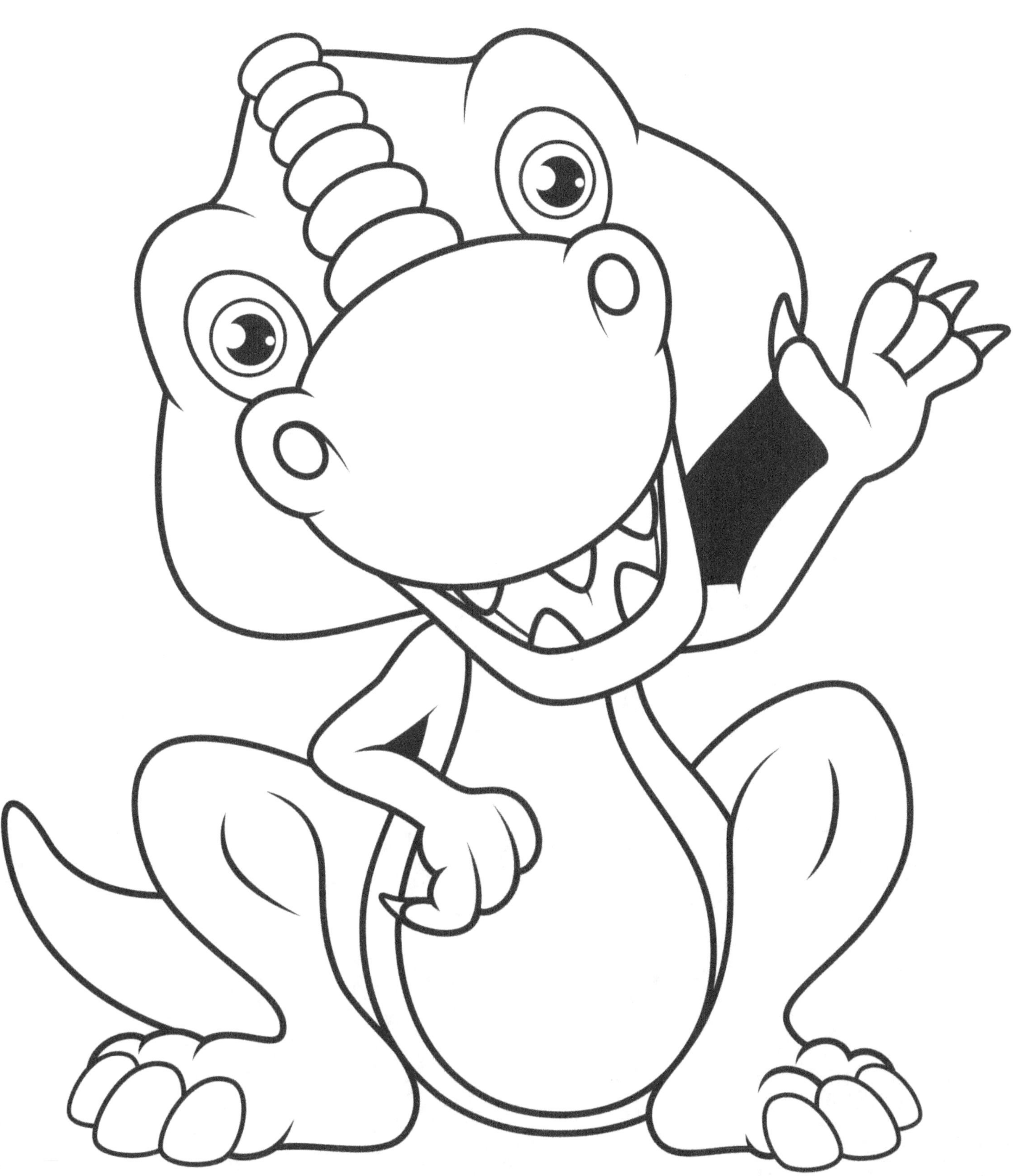